First published in the Un
National Maternity Sup
23 Turpir
Wel ,
Hertfordshire
AL6 0RP
www.jakescharity.org
NMSF is a registered charity, no. 1118833

© National Maternity Support Foundation (NMSF)

Little Book of Happy Memories copyright © National Maternity Support Foundation (NMSF)

Author: Andrew Canter

All rights reserved. No part of this publication may be reproduced, stored in a retrieval system, or transmitted, in any form or by any means, electronic, mechanical, photocopying, recording or otherwise, without the prior written permission of the National Maternity Support Foundation (NMSF).

Illustrations and images supplied by the children of Oaklands Primary School, Welwyn, Maria Floyd and with the kind permission of Watford Football Club

ISBN: 978152404607

In memory of our little Star

For Rachel, Ruby, Mia and Theo

Dear Bridie

Hope you enjoy all of the 'happy memories'

With best wishes

Andrew

Foreword

I am delighted and honoured to introduce you to a wonderful collection of happy childhood memories. I have been really impressed by NMSF's great work to help improve maternity care over the past few years.

They have shown that by recognising the incredible work of midwives and awarding them a scholarship in the challenging area of bereavement care makes such a positive difference to parents and their families.

I am pleased and proud to be part of their journey and helping them as a Patron of the charity.

Natasha Kaplinsky OBE, Broadcaster and NMSF Patron

About NMSF

National Maternity Support Foundation (NMSF), also known as Jake's Charity was set up following the tragic stillbirth of Jake Canter due to the nearest Hospital maternity unit being closed. NMSF strives to achieve significant improvement in maternity care.

We continue to work closely with NHS Trusts to ensure that maternity units are kept safe, accessible and well resourced. We work in partnership with many organisations and in particular, the Royal College of Midwives (RCM), the professional body of Midwives and consult with them on issues surrounding maternity care.

Through *Jake's Scholarship* we continue to support and train midwives in the challenging area of bereavement care.

Andrew Canter, Chairman, NMSF
Rachel Canter, Chief Executive, NMSF

National Caring Week

> great care = positive experience = happy memory

National Caring Week was launched in partnership with our local school, Oaklands Primary School in Welwyn, Hertfordshire, where our three children, Ruby, Mia and Theo attend.

It ran from Saturday 29th October to Friday 4th November 2016 to coincide with *National Maternity Day*, marking Jake's anniversary.

The whole school were asked to suggest 'Caring Activities' for which the children and parents were sponsored. This was a great success and there are plans to replicate this nationally and encourage more schools to get involved.

To ensure there was a permanent record for National Caring Week, we produced this *Little Book of Happy Memories*. The children created drawings, paintings, sketches of their favourite childhood memories – the year winners are featured within.

We hope you enjoy all of the happy memories.

Oaklands School: Reception - Winner

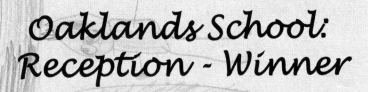

"When it was my birthday, I had a party and I went on a bouncy castle"

Erin Whinnett

The Long Journey

My cousins lived a few miles away and we would see them regularly. We always wanted to have sleepovers and would plead with our parents to let us stay together, especially if we had been visiting them for the day.

So one game we used to play was to hide in the car for the entire journey and then jump out when we reached home. Of course the parents knew fully well what we were up to, but would play along with it.

The idea of a child travelling in the floor well of a car would be unthinkable nowadays, but it seemed perfectly okay back then.

The Rt Hon Grant Shapps, MP for Welwyn Hatfield and NMSF Patron

Lost and Found

When I was 6 years old I got lost on holiday in Magaluf. I was a little bit scared and looked everywhere for my family for what seemed like ages.

I went to all the places I thought my family would be, but without success. Eventually I thought my best chance would be to go back to our apartment. So I sat on the step for a few hours. Suddenly I saw my Dad.

He ran towards me picked me up and didn't let go. All I remember is my Dad saying "choose a toy, anything you want".

Well that was that, happy days! I got a cap gun that was so loud and so brilliant. It all turned out rather well in the end - everyone was happy!

Andrew Canter, Chairman, NMSF (Jake's Dad)

School Pick-Up

My sister and I would look forward to the one day of the week when our Grandad picked us up from school, Catton Grove Primary School, in Norfolk.

Grandad was fun loving and generous and drove a little black van and we'd bundle in the back, no seats let alone seat belts and be greeted by "Kipper" Nana and Grandad's dog. We'd often go straight to Mousehold Heath to take Kipper for a long walk, stopping to climb on our "monkey" tree or run full pelt down the mounds or I'd play with my imaginary friend or dog.

On the way back to my Nana and Grandad's home we'd stop off at the local newsagents "Aubrey's" to choose penny sweets we'd have to count up. My Grandad was a well-liked local often chatting to people he knew in the shop which is lovely but we had to wait until we left the shop before we could eat our sweets- sometimes it felt like an eternity!

We'd be greeted with a big hug and a lovely prepared tea by my Nana at their house. We'd be allowed to watch TOTP all of us dancing to the chart music. Sometimes we'd have sleepovers at theirs, my sister and I sharing a big double bed, chatting and giggling into the night!!

Next day we'd spend many hours in Grandad's workshop playing shops or schools or walking Kipper up and down the lane. Such carefree, happy times.

Rachel Canter, Chief Executive, NMSF (Jake's Mum)

Picnic-By-The-Sea

Two strong memories come to mind about my childhood from the mid-1950s. Living in Norfolk, not far from the coast, my parents would nearly always pack a picnic on a Sunday (Norfolk scones, made by my mother, were an obligatory part of the picnic) and we would head off to the coast, where we would meet up with my Aunts, Uncles and cousins.

Mundesley was a favourite spot, as we could park our car on the cliff top and walk down to the beach. My father taught me to swim in the sea, although you had to be very careful as the undercurrent at Mundesley could be very strong, but once the tide was out, large pools of sea water were left there for all sorts of fun.

After our cliff top picnic a game of Rounder's was played, then the short drive home and bed. What a wonderful, happy memory that is, and of course it was always sunny!

Eileen Burrows (Jake's Nanna)

Seeing the New Queen

My other memory was of seeing the new Queen Elizabeth II in 1954.

After the Queen was crowned in 1953, she did a tour of Britain, visiting many cities and towns.

My mother took my brother and myself to see the grand car drive slowly along the streets of Norwich to the City Hall.

The Duke of Edinburgh was with her, and us children all had flags to wave and a day off school!

Eileen Burrows (Jake's Nanna)

Slip Sliding Away

I am very lucky as I had an amazing childhood with so many wonderful memories so it is really hard to pick one but here goes.

We used to go to Knebworth a lot with my cousins in the school holidays and have a big picnic. I loved playing cricket with them, my brothers & my Dad.

Mum usually busied herself making sure we had enough to eat & drink. It was great walking up the steps of the massive slide with our mats and then sitting on the mats & whizzing down to the bottom.

And being a tomboy I thought the adventure playground was brilliant too.

Louise Bronstein (Jake's Auntie)

Smarties at the Summit

We were a family of four children and, often on a Sunday, we would go out walking.

I always remember going up a hill when I was about six (I think it was called Humbledon Hill) and at some point my father disappeared.

He came back and as we approached the summit said "There are sometimes fairies at the top of this hill. They leave things for children who have managed the climb."

Of course, we all then raced to the summit where, with great glee, we found four packets of *Smarties*.

I loved the idea of the fairies at the top of the hill!

Professor Cathy Warwick CBE, Chief Executive, Royal College of Midwives and NMSF Lead Patron

Cheating at Monopoly

Sitting under Tok's wooden veranda during school holidays playing the same game of Monopoly for days on end with my cousins (no idea how we managed to always stretch the games out so much!) whilst sucking on Assam sweets that were so sour you couldn't help but pull the stupidest faces as you sucked them. Think my being banker and cheating like a pro by siphoning off the cash under the board must have helped my winning streak!

Driving my aunt's brand new car around and around in Tok's garden, at the tender age of 11. Hours of fun!

Playing in the gutter(!) and scooping out tadpoles and frogs with our fishing nets.

Playing Huckleberry Finn with my best friend (Tom Sawyer, of course) and 'catching fish' with a string on a pole, with a 'flip flop' (aka 'fish') tied onto the end of it.

Annette Pendrey

Sport for Life

I really liked all my life sports. When I was young my parents sent me and my brother to a youth sport camp during summer for getting every chance to do all the sports we wanted to with kids we never meet before. We really liked two weeks of surfing, football, swimming , rowing, tennis, etc and as well getting in touch with different kind of interesting kids with different backgrounds.

Sebastian Prödl, Premier League Footballer, Watford FC

Cops 'n Robbers

Being 8 years old and growing up in North Yorkshire. We lived in a Close with lots of other families. They were the times when we could go and call on them to see if they wanted to play. Caroline, Louise, Nathan, Diane, Christopher, my brother Dom and I. We would take our make-shift go-carts to the top of the 'tarmac path' and wizz all the way to the bottom.

There was a Beck (stream) that ran along the bottom of our Close from one end to a field of cows where I first discovered what a 'cow pat' was! I can't believe that we were allowed down there on our own - the freedom that we had.

There was a small corner shop at the top of the road where we would spend our pocket money on our favourite sweets - Parma Violets, Refreshers, Gob Stoppers, Black Jacks. We'd play 'Cops 'n Robbers' in the garden and revive those that had been "shot" with a sweet! Making perfume with fallen petals from Rose bushes. Putting them in jam jars with water and letting them ferment and then giving them to our Mums!

Corine Pendry

Love and Laughter

Growing up the youngest of four girls was never lonely. The house was always full of people and noise.

We weren't well off in the slightest but the house was always full of love and laughter. Neighbours, cousins, friends it always seemed full of activity.

Simple pleasures like playing outside with a gang of others on our bikes, playing marbles, skipping or elastic skipping!?!?

The sun always seemed to shine. Learning to ride my bike when my sisters pushed me down a hill, playing kerbs and literally spending all day outside somewhere.

Freedom and friends, happy sunny days.

Caroline Reed

A 'Tasty' Snake

I grew up in Thailand which seems totally normal to me because all my friends also grew up in Thailand. However, with hindsight, I realise there were some differences, such as the local wildlife.

One summer holiday at the beach, I walked out of the holiday house (think beach bungalow on stilts) to join my family on the sand. I was passed by a large snake, slithering as snakes do, the other way along the path. I remember it being easily twice as long as I was tall, so I'm going to say it was 2 metres long, although you're welcome to assume an element of exaggeration.

I responded exactly as I'd been taught – I turned to face the snake and then calmly walked away from it, while it continued on its peaceful journey towards and then under the bungalow. Naturally, I was keen to share all the details of this encounter with my family. My parents, unsure what type of snake I'd seen (and I certainly was no help here), were concerned that it had taken residence under the bungalow and reported the incident to the housekeeper, Pob.

Pob took the matter very seriously, spent his afternoon seeking out the beast and was proud to inform my parents that the snake had duly been found ... and killed. My concerned parents thanked him profusely, relieved to hear that Pob had gone to such lengths to ensure our safety. After all, this must have been a dangerous snake if it had been necessary to kill it.

Not at all, Pob told them with a large smile. This was not a dangerous snake at all. However, it was edible and he was delighted to say that he was cooking it for our dinner that night.

Lindsay Smith

Man's Best Friend

Moving house is stressful for adults but for five-year-old me it felt like a disaster. My life had been centred on a familiar back lane teeming with dozens of kids who were an extended family to me, always there to involve me in their games or to take care of me.

Overnight, my world contracted to our new, quiet street where the few children around seemed hostile and unwelcoming. And as far as I could see, my parents didn't understand any of this. But they did, of course.

A few days after we moved, I heard my Dad arrive home from his work in the shipyard. As usual, before I could see him I could smell him: the familiar and not unpleasant scent of lathe oil permeated the all-in-one overalls he always wore for work.

I remember the scene perfectly. He walked in with a smile bigger than usual and a small bulge in his chest. Undoing his top buttons, a small, furry head popped out and fixed me with his brown eyes. A Staffordshire bull terrier puppy, only weeks old.

Spike, named after the dog from 'Tom and Jerry', became my best friend for the next 14 years. Always happy to play, to protect me from bullies and to be cuddled.

We were inseparable and he didn't leave me until I was at University and his job was done. To this day, I think of him when I need a friend. Or when I smell lathe oil.

Professor Brian Smith

School milk and Puff the Magic Dragon

Memories of a 5 year old boy. My first year at infant school was 1966. At that time during morning class everyone was given a small bottle of milk to drink. I did not like milk, but the bottle had to be finished before playtime so I always managed to finish it, if somewhat reluctantly. One day our teacher told us we were going to make a dragon – not any dragon, but Puff the Magic Dragon.

The class excitement could not be contained. To build Puff the Magic Dragon took special things: card board boxes, chicken wire, Papier Mache, paint and the magic ingredient – milk bottle tops. I still remember collecting and washing all the used silver milk bottle tops that would be used for the dragon's scales. It took numbers of days to gather enough to cover the dragon. Even those, myself included, who did not like milk did their part by drinking our milk quickly.

When finished Puff our mighty dragon was the pride of the class he was the finest dragon in the land. One day I came to school and Puff was no more it had disappeared. Some say he slipped back into his cave. We believed the teacher when we were told he was safe because as we all know dragons live forever. So now even now after 50 years occasionally I think of my long lost friend Puff and smile - that's of course when I see a milk bottle top

Mike Reynolds

A Truly Happy Time

I grew up in Lancashire. Money was scarce after the second world war so we did not often go away on holiday and if we did it was to the Lake District.

The second of the two holidays we had was to Broughton-in-Furness to stay at the High Cross Inn.

Last year nearly seventy years later I travelled from Barrow to Whitehaven as part of the National Maternity Review and on the way we passed the same High Cross Inn apparently unchanged, still painted a yellow/cream colour and all my memories of a truly happy time came back. I couldn't wait to phone my sister.

Thank you to Jake's Charity for all your good work.

Sir Cyril Chantler, FRCP FRCPCH FMedSci, Vice Chairman, National Maternity Review

Oaklands School: Year Two - Winner

"Sri Lanka houses to stay for 30 days"

Aqeel Fauz

On Your Bike

I remember fondly the morning a letter arrived on the mat, inside the front door, addressed to me. I had won a bike! I was 11 years old and recall bounding up the stairs and bouncing on my parent's bed with excitement.

Weeks earlier I had entered a Spot-the-Difference Competition, posted by a local business called *Castlemahon Chickens*, on the *Limerick Leader* newspaper.

There were two almost identical pictures of a man in his stripy pyjamas peering hungrily into an open fridge full of food, some of which was chicken. I can still visualise those pictures. I soon spotted the ten differences, marked them, posted my entry and...some weeks later heard I had won the bike!

When the day came to collect my winnings I donned my best outfit: a rust-coloured knee length dress with white knee socks and my favourite 'Starsky and Hutch' style belted knit cardigan (it was 1976!), I still have somewhere the yellowing newspaper cutting of the photo of me and the bike. It appeared that very week in the next edition of the paper. My prize was a Raleigh shopper. The frame was metallic blue, it had a white saddle and hand grips. It was brand new and it was all mine. I loved that bike.

Marie Reynolds

Flaming Brilliant

November 5th - Fireworks night was always a night to look forward to. I lived on an avenue full of very big oak trees and at this time of the year all the leaves were falling off the trees which made fantastic stuffing for our 'Guys'!!

My brother and I used to get old clothes from our parents and once the bottom of the trouser legs were tied we used to stuff the trousers with the leaves. We both made our own 'Guy', a bit of a completion really. Once they were made we put a mask on their faces and they lived in the shed until bonfire night!

Our bonfire was always big. My dad used to bring old wood home from work and we all built the bonfire. My dad took us to the shops to buy fireworks and we carefully selected each one ourselves. We kept them in a tin in the bottom of the airing cupboard - not a safe place I now think!

Firework night and the 'Guys' were put on the bonfire and then it was lit. All of our friends came and my dad lit the fireworks which were amazing and lit up the skies with big sparkles and bangs! A brilliant time was had by us all!

Anne Graveling

Let it Snow

It may seem strange that someone like me, who nowadays loves to be warm and sit in the sun, has a favourite childhood memory about snowy winters which were the 'norm' when I was a growing lad.

It wasn't really about the snow itself, it was about a couple of things you could do in the snow, which were unlike anything else we experienced. Firstly, it was about making slides: we used to make slides on any flat surface so long as there was enough snow (about 3-4 inches): in the playground; in the road; on the path and especially down any suitable slope. The more we slid, the slippery it became; the slippery it became, the longer the slide. Grown-ups didn't like them – but did we care? Of course not.

Secondly, it was about sledging. Sledges in those days were small homemade wooden structures, with either steel or aluminium runners, polished with candle wax. I lived close to the top, of what was considered, the steepest hill in Norwich. It was so steep that it took me until I was about 15 before I could bike up it and that was only by zig-zagging up the steepest parts. If we had lots of snow this hill was free from traffic, and became the ultimate challenge for me and my mates to sledge down; but even more of a challenge to climb up afterwards, pulling our sledges. Happy days……

Roger Burrows (Jake's Grandad)

Our Magic Forest

Growing up in Nigeria in the early 80's, was so much fun. There were a whole lot of fun experiences and that saying it takes a village to raise a child was very apt back then. There were no computers, iPads, very limited TV shows. Children actually played in the neighbourhood and made friends, communication and direct interaction was all we had back then. I vividly remember growing up and actually having so much respect for older folks even if you had never seen the person, once you see an older person you had to greet, some of the older people really took that and ran with it, the unwritten rule was for them to discipline any child they thought was out of order, even if they had no inkling who the parents of that child was.

It was always fun especially during holidays, making so much from nothing. I learnt how to crochet, how to plait hair, how to make racing cars out of empty sugar cartons and broom sticks, and we would have a full competition on whose car moved the fastest. We moved around with no fear or care in the world, and once it was getting dark and the street lights came on we had to be at home. I recall one period in time, there was an abandoned piece of land, with the sand around that area being red like crimson. We would pretend like we were cooking, with empty tins of milk; we would mix sand and water and pretend serving it like a proper meal and graduated to one of us actually stealing match sticks from home and lighting fires.

Then one very day someone suggested we go look for where to buy fish hooks, I remember telling my dad to please help me get some hooks, he asked why, and I said we found fish in our stream, and he said what stream and I said our stream that flows in our forest. He probably thought I was crazy, but believe me we all thought we owned that land. Some of the lucky kids actually ended up catching fishes. I was unlucky I never caught any. They roasted it, and we all shared it. These are just a few of my childhood memories growing up in Lagos Nigeria. Writing this has really brought about some nostalgic feelings. I have since lost touch with most of the kids I grew up with, but writing these I can put a face and a voice to every character that helped shape my childhood.

Halle Aworinde

Digging to Australia

I grew up in a lane where many members of my extended family also had houses - and my childhood is packed full of happy memories of playing outside together at the end of a long summer's day. Riding my bike up and down the lane, digging 'all the way to Australia' in a nearby field, racing my sister and cousins in the front garden, playing ball up against the wall at the back of the house, and then going inside for pop and crisps!

Throughout, my parents believed in me, and filled me with confidence everyday - and it is their words I still hear as a 40 year-old woman - running two hospitals and leading maternity transformation across England.

Sarah-Jane Marsh, Chief Executive of Birmingham Children's Hospital and Birmingham Women's Hospital, Chair of the new Maternity Transformation Programme Board

Teatime Treats
by Clare Luther

Down a wide leafy road with a London postcode, lived my grandparents - Galee and Gramps. They were caring and kind, and both sound in mind; these people were my childhood champs. Every time I went in I was greeted with grins that stretched right across their soft faces.

Together we'd huddle for a kiss and a cuddle; their home was my favourite of places. Gramps walked through the hall, with a clock that stood tall, to sit in his comfy green seat. As he flopped in his chair he would talk without care, whilst Galee got us nibbles to eat.

Teatime Treats
by Clare Luther

Their little brown dog, who was shaped like a log, would beg to be on Gramps's lap. Sitting still by his feet she longed for his seat, and whined with a mighty high yap.

But the dog was ignored until tea was poured, and the biscuits and sweets all came out. The choice was quite small yet I wanted them all; how I loved this time, without doubt. As Gramps sipped his tea, the brown dog on his knee would lick his ten fingers all round.

Teatime Treats
by Clare Luther

I remember it now, like last week somehow - this odd habit he shared with his hound. Gramps spread his hands wide as she licked every side, then handed me a teatime treat.

I would widen my eyes in complete surprise as wet fingers passed the biscuits to eat!

By Clare Luther, Author of Happy To Be Me, Safari Series/Illustrations by Maria Floyd

Dodging PC Roberts

Hours of street footy, endlessly kicking a ball against the garden wall alone or trying to score against brother Nick in the garage door goal.

Street cricket with the lamp-post as the wicket and the thrill of bowling out Willie Davenport who was 5 years older than me.

Endless abortive attempts to beat 'Shrimp' Johnson's record of riding a tricycle on two wheels around our block, which measured some 400 yards round the square.

Dodging PC Roberts on his Velocette motorbike as he tried to catch me cycling on the pavement whilst on my paper round.

Listening to (and being frightened by) 'Journey into Space' on an old crystal wireless set under the bedclothes after lights out.

Cycling round to Grandpa's house to watch 'The Lone Ranger' on a 1950's black and white square television.

Watching with anticipation as Granny Ella (my Scottish paternal grandmother) made sure that the silver sixpences wrapped in greaseproof paper found their way into the Christmas pudding about to be dished up.

Excitedly pushing my hand to the bottom of my Christmas stocking, pinned to the bottom of my bed, to reveal a silver sixpence, a tangerine and a Dinky toy.

Barry and Linda Varnon

Staying Up Late

It was when the French football team won the World Cup in 1998. I was 10 years old and it was a late kick-off, and my parents let me watch the game. I was so happy to watch to the end and was able to celebrate with them after the game so my memory was a very happy one.

Etienne Capoue, Premier League Footballer, Watford FC

A '70s Christmas

Looking back with a smile at Christmas time growing up in the 1970s....

The forever-lasting Woolworths Christmas tree decorated with as many baubles as it could hold, no theme or colour scheme necessary. Tinsel embracing each and every item on the wall and foil lanterns hanging from the ceiling. The Advent Calendar we looked forward to opening so much, even though it was only a picture behind each window.

Mum and I, seated and braced with nut crackers in hand, ready to shell the nut selection whilst watching classic TV; Scrooge, Chitty Chitty Bang Bang, The Sound of Music and the obligatory James Bond. Babycham and Cherry B for the grown-ups, and a Snowball for me.....

Andie Doyle

The Sound of Music

A childhood obsession with the sound of music and singing along to music was the reason for the many times when my Mum and me would have a home musical extravaganza!

We would dress up in her old lace petticoats and hats and dance and sing around the house to the songs and music as loud as the old record player would let it go.

The *Lonely Goatherd* was always a big favourite that we danced and sang to over and over again.

Tchaikovsky's 'Swan Lake' was our other big favourite again very good to dance to in skirts that flowed and very theatrical. Such happy memories

Jo Watt, Lead Community Midwife and NMSF Patron

All The Fun of The Fair

As we approached the fun fair, the sight, sound and smell filled me with excitement. I could see more than my older siblings because my father gave me a 'piggy back shoulder ride'. I was fit to burst with emotion.

My favourite ride was the pirate ship. As the ride moved back and forth, my sister and I screamed with excitement. I glanced behind me and saw the strong powerful frame of my father.

In one hand he had a strong grip of the net that encircled the ride. His other hand had a firm grip on me! Secure in the hands of my father, I remember willing the ship to swing higher.

Professor Jacqueline Dunkley-Bent OBE, Head of Maternity, Children and Young People, NHS England

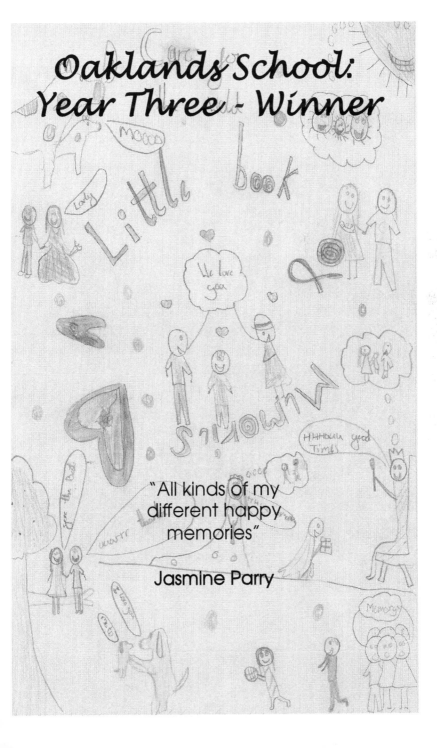

Cooling Down at The Lido

Living in the Midlands we were about as far away as one could possibly be from the seaside.

Fortunately, we had lovely Sutton Park nearby, which had an outdoor pool.

My brother and I and our friends spent many a hot, sunny Sunday afternoon picnicking in the park and cooling down in 'The Lido' as it was called back then.

The highlight of the day was the journey home, ice lolly in hand, listening to the radio and singing along to the 'top twenty' countdown on Radio One and trying to guess what the No 1 song would be that week!"

Samantha Collinge, Bereavement Support Specialist Midwife and Jake's Midwife

Ready for Take Off

It was July 1979, I was 7 and I was going on a plane for the first time, in fact my older siblings and my parents were all going on a plane for the very first time too. I felt the nervous excitement build in the family as we approached the airport, I wasn't nervous, I was just in awe of the whole experience. I remember everything about the holiday, the fact we couldn't sit together on the plane and I had to hold my mums hand across the aisle as we taxied down the runway, I knew then that she was more nervous than me, I remember the hotel, in what was then Yugoslavia, the fact we didn't like the food in the hotel so went outside for chips and ice cream every night, the joy of the sunshine (I am from the North of England!), being in the pool all day, every day, the Japanese kids I befriended and spending real quality time with my family and all the laughs that came with it.

Before this day I can't recall being that enthused about anything else, not in a bad way, I was a happy and blessed child. I just didn't love sports or school or have any particular hobbies, but that holiday changed everything, I fell in love with the adventure, the sunshine, the swimming, the fun, the excitement, the different smells and tastes that come from travelling and the total escape from everyday life that you get from being on holiday. From that day forward I learnt everything I could about holidays and became such a geek that by the age of 10 I could advise the travel agent of other hotel options in a particular Mediterranean resort if the 'computer said no'. I know a total geek!

I didn't realise it then but I now see that holiday as a sort of sliding door moment in my life, that led to a life-long passion for travel that has seen me leave school at 16 to become a travel agent, then study Tourism at Uni, backpack around the world, secure dream jobs in tour operators and airlines, fall in love with Australia, marry an amazing man who loves travel as much as I do, emigrate and now promote the country I love to people all over the world, including the UK, here I hope my work also ignites the passion in other 7 year old kids as they go on holiday for the first time!

Robin Mack

TV for The First Time

A very happy memory from my childhood was when I watched TV for the first time, when I was seven years old. It was a cartoon from Japan I think or something like that. It was black and white as well! I was so happy that I had the opportunity to watch TV because I had never had that before, because I was born on a farm and we moved to a town a little later and we didn't have TV before so that was great for me.

Heurelho Gomes, Premier League Footballer, Watford FC

Worth Waiting For

Most summers were spent holidaying in the north of Spain. This special memory is ignited and relived simply by the smell of a rotisserie chicken. It's amazing the power a smell can have to transport you back to a time and a place...

The nearest beach was over two hour away, so whenever we went, we would spend the day playing in the hot sun, eating sardines grilled in a beach side restaurant for lunch and playing some more.

For me the return journey home and the reward of a rotisserie chicken was the cherry on the cake. It always happened on the way home, after spending a long day in the sea and in the sun, and it was always split in two stops. On the first one we enjoyed fresh water from the fountain, water that travelled from the mountains, so cold and clear and deliciously quenching.

The second stop was our dinner. The showstopper! Oh how I couldn't wait to tear the chicken with my hands and feast on it till full and sleepy. I recall the lay by we pulled into and the chickens cooking, turning slowly.

The aroma filled the car, just like that strong fish and chips smell you get as you rush home to feast, tempted and mouth watering. I couldn't wait to indulge and to this day it never disappoints.

Liz Malyon (née Liston)

A Passion for Fun and Curiosity

Moving from a concrete, grey, insect infested, dirty Deptford to the luscious, surroundings of Wimbledon, where ever corner dripped in varying shades of green and the bright blue sky felt so close, expansive and touchable, was a blessing from above. We had moved to paradise! And paradise was just a hop, skip and a jump from the wonders of Wimbledon Common!

Mum and dad lavished us with love and three other special ingredients – imagination, energy and attention. Our favourite games involved exploring and seeking, usually for Wombles – for years we were convinced that only Mum and Dad could see them because we were never quick enough or quiet enough – we'd always scare them off back under the ground. My little brother was quite short for his age and extremely mischievous. Amazingly, on one visit we lost him in in a snow-drift, filled ditch, whilst we were running after our dad.

WHOOSH! He disappeared up to his neck. Our childhood was crammed full of lazy days lying on the soft carpets of green, making dens out of old, brittle wood and hiding in the crunchy leaf filled slopes. As we grew older, we even pretended be our favourite heroes or heroines like Wonder Woman or Evil Knievel and the common always had a special role to play; for example, we would whizz on my brother's racer bike, down the mountainous hills that lay silent like the back of a sleeping dinosaur and our roars of laughter would echo far into the surrounding, densely packed trees.

I wouldn't swap my childhood for all the tea in china! It nurtured my love of the outdoors, adventure, awe and wonder. It made me believe that anything is possible with a dash of imagination, good company and enthusiasm. I've passed this infectious passion for fun and an overwhelming sense of curiosity, on to my own children. We visit the common regularly and the rush of nostalgia every time we visit is almost indescribable.

Tracey Eaden

Listen to Your Dad

My dad was a family doctor in Colombo, Sri Lanka. From the moment that I was born he wanted me to be a lady doctor.

As a child he inspired me by taking me to his country practice once a week and thrilling me with glorious stories about saving lives as a young doctor at the general hospital.

My special memory is of my dad asking me to stand on a chair by his side as he examined a pregnant mother and he taught me how to listen to the fetal heart.

I was just 5 years old.

Dr Gowri Motha, Gentle Birth Method

Childhood Treats

My happy memories of childhood revolve mostly around food. Dad would take me swimming, which was always exciting, especially when the giant inflatables were in the pool. However, the best bit was when Dad would say I could spend the 10p he'd given me for the locker in the sweet machine in the foyer. I would always get 'Tootie Frooties'. The sugar rush when I was tired and probably still a little damp, made them taste even better.

Mum provided the home made treats, which usually involved the added benefit of licking the mixing bowl, my contribution to helping. Mum would make wonderful scones, which went with my Gran's amazing 'freezer strawberry jam'. I was never quite sure why it was called that, although if there was a glut of strawberries from the garden then the freezer certainly would be full of small pots of jam. Family social occasions, which were sometimes tense, would suddenly become easier in the presence of home baking.

These are happy memories because they were relatively infrequent. Having sweets really was a rare treat and one to be savoured – it's amazing how long a 10p penny mix could be made to last. And now, in 'middle-age', I'm glad my parents taught me the power of a treat, something I don't have every day which then becomes something special, to be remembered with a smile on my face.

Sarah Ward

A Clumsy Ballerina

My childhood memory is how incredibly awkward I always was. This was never more apparent than when I was privileged enough to attend ballet classes. I sensed on entering the class for the first time that I was not destined nor had any desire to be a ballerina.

Covent Garden held no enticement. Having realised my lack of interest and motivation I set out to sabotage the classes by deliberately doing the wrong steps and encouraging the rest of the class to do likewise.

My behaviour was so disruptive that the teacher eventually asked my mother to remove me from her lessons and as an unprecedented incentive offered her a full refund on the class fees!

I can't say that I ever regretted my behaviour but was somewhat sorry for the embarrassment I caused my mother!

Debbie Wall

Oaklands School:
Year Four - Winner

"Me and my uncle building my first lego set at my nans! (we spent hours!)"

"Me and my best friend Lily had a birthday sleep-over and we had soo much fun!"

"It was Christmas and we got stink bugs in our stockings they stunk (we were in Miller's bedroom so he had to smell it!) also we woke up at 2.00am"

Souki Smith

Dressing Up for Fun

One of my happiest childhood memories is of the dressing-up box – a large trunk full of the most amazing old clothes, curtains, shoes and hats that had been collected over many years.

The five of us children would rummage about and dress up in anything from pre-war outfits to square-dancing skirts from the 1950s.

Then we would put on plays for the adults or just dance – whirling round and round to the music from the record player, sometimes inside and sometimes outside, but always blissfully happy.

Dr Clea Harmer, Chief Executive, Sands

If You Go Down to the Woods Today

My mother and her antiquated turquoise Austin motorcar with leopard print seat covers took us miraculously from Wokingham in Berks to The New Forest without breaking down. Such joy when we reached our campsite in the woods, so excited to sleep outdoors in a tent and as kids we had no idea that our borrowed camping equipment was budget so say the least.

Our first sleep was…well let's say different as our fern filled pillow cases gathered from the forest were a tad lumpy and we were interrupted from horses sniffing and kicking around but we kind of got used to it and it made us giggle.

We stopped off every morning to get a French stick from the local bakery and mum would fill it with pate for our picnic on the beach, the sun shone as it always seemed to when you are a child. We had the best time ever, just the 3 of us and our modest tent and of course daily ice creams plus my brother met a nice girl from Bath called Tracy!

Stephanie Larkinson

Seeing Ninja Turtles in Blackpool!

Going to Blackpool with all my family. We got a coach up, like a school bus, and the whole family went up for the weekend, there was about 27 of us! I was about five or six and the Ninja Turtles were there and it was one of the best things ever! I got a Ninja Turtles 50 pence piece and I never lost it! That would be my favourite memory just because everyone was there and for all the family to be together.

Troy Deeney, Premier League Footballer, Watford FC

Getting 'Plastered' At the Pool

From as early as I can remember most of my summer holidays were spent at the Ely Outdoor pool. Membership was 50p from May to September. There was very little health and safety in those days. I would charge around the pool bombing and diving, racing from one side to the other, climbing out and repeat the process. Plasters were always at hand due to cut feet. Once plastered I would carry on playing. I would run up the grass banks and dive in, with grass still on my feet, which would follow me into the pool.

In fact the majority of my summer was spent in a swimsuit, no matter the weather. Heavy rain would just make jumping off the diving board more daring. By the end of each day I was absolutely knackered with chlorine-wrinkled fingers, bleached hair and if I wasn't careful, a mild sunburn. However it was all worth it as a glistening light bulb would occasionally be turned on which always seemed to be at the other end of the pool. I would swim as fast as I could, heave my puppy fat body out of the pool, roll over and sprint to the cafe for an ice cream. I always felt that I deserved it.

Cate Jackson

Watching the Big Match-with Chocolate

My happy childhood memory was travelling from North West London to see my Grandparents every Sunday in Ilford. It doesn't seem far but this was before the days of the M25.

My routine was the same every week, head straight for their "secret" chocolate stash in their sideboard (always in the top drawer) and then settle down to watch "The Big Match" hosted by Brian Moore with my Poppa whilst my Dad slept in another room.

Being a Dad now myself I totally understand why.

Marc Kirsch

Outdoor Adventure

One of my favourite childhood memories was when my dad took me camping for the first time. We drove for what seemed was an age - but was only really about half an hour away from home - set up our tent and cooked spaghetti hoops and sausages on the gas cooker.

It was great to spend time with my dad just the two of us.

The overriding memory from that trip though was learning to cross the road - I wouldn't cross except when there was no sign of any cars, despite my dad smiling and beckoning me across!

Joe Bronstein

'Knickerbocker Glory' Days

Some of my happiest memories as a child were when we went on holiday to Scotland. My parents used to love to go to the Scottish Borders and Jedburgh in particular. I remember the journey well, sat in the back with a toy steering wheel, pretending to drive us through Otterburn, over Carter Bar and into Jedburgh.

When we were there, I used to love to play cricket with my Dad next to Jedburgh Abbey and hit many a six! Then after all the fun of the day, we would go back to the hotel for tea and I could have my favourite treat that I only got on holiday.

I had to stand on the chair to eat it so I could reach the top of the glass, but I loved to end the day with a knickerbocker glory! Happy days!

Peter Shippey, Co-Founder of The Shippey Campaign

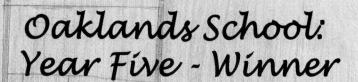

Oaklands School: Year Five - Winner

"This is about me and my mum scuba diving at Kho Mak"

Willow Bonar

A Warm Feeling at Disney World

I lost my mum when I was only 7 and one of my happiest memories is when we went to Disney World the year before she died.

I remember being on the 'Spinning Teacups' ride with the whole family, laughing so much I could barely keep my head up as we went round-and-round. I remember closing my eyes and feeling the warm sun on my face.

Pure childhood bliss.

Jenny Gregory, Bereavement Midwife, Northumbria Healthcare NHS Foundation Trust and Jake's Midwife

Endless Fun at the 'Family Gathering'

I was lucky that the extended family arranged a reunion once a year in a holiday resort. It was an occasion that we all dreamed of and prepared for several months in advance. Over 20 children of different ages staying together for 2 weeks was a memorable experience. We had many stories to share and many activities to enjoy.

There was not a minute to lose and only few hours of sleep, we had to fit in cycling, sailing, swimming, table tennis, board games and many other activities into the program. However; the highlight of our vacation was to play pranks on parents that on occasions led to unexpected results.

When in trouble, love, loyalty, friendships and solidarity became more apparent.

Mr Rami K Atalla, Senior Consultant Obstetrician and Gynaecologist, MB, ChB, MRCOG and NMSF Patron

Acknowledgements

We would like to thank Natasha Kaplinsky for her kind words contained within the foreword. Also great thanks to, Children's Author, Clare Luther for her brilliant poem and Maria Floyd for her lovely illustrations.

A special thank you to Julie Petitt and Matthew Hudson, and all the children and parents from Oaklands School for their support throughout for National Caring Week and brilliant drawings.

A huge thank you to everyone that have shared their wonderful happy childhood memories.

Last but by no means least, thank you to all of our family and friends for their continued support.

Clare Luther & Maria Floyd

Maria Floyd, illustrator, and Clare Luther, author, are both passionate about creating stories that help children recognise and relate to their own experiences. They have published two sets of books in the Safari Series - both sets contain three books held in their own gift case. Each brightly illustrated book is written in humorous rhyme, that deliver easy lessons in English language reading and comprehension, with a thoughtful moral and fun facts about Africa's best loved creatures. The Savanna Set tells of being happy as you are, the importance of friendship, and treating others as you would like to be treated. The Okavango Set tells of working better together as a team, thinking before you speak and accepting others for who they are (not judging). Their third set, The Red Desert Set, is due in print early July '17 and tells of putting others first, perseverance, and the act of kindness winning through.

E: tallgrassbooks@outlook.com/
FB: Tall Grass Productions - Facebook.com/tallgrassbooks/
T: @tallgrassHQ

Clare Luther studied Occupational Therapy at Oxford Brookes University. She worked as an Occupational Therapist and Life Coach, in both the public and private sector, until 2013. Clare now has a diverse work life where she continues to use her skills in a variety of settings. She has held a passion for writing poetry since her teenage years. She lives in London with her husband and two children.

Maria Floyd studied Fine Art and History of Art at Goldsmiths' College, London and is a successful painter and illustrator. She has held several exhibitions of her work in the UK and divides her time between Devon and North Cornwall. She lives with her husband and three children.

Disclaimer

This book is designed to provide information and motivation to our readers. It is sold with the understanding that the publisher is not engaged to render any type of psychological, legal, or any other kind of professional advice. The content of each 'happy memory' is the sole expression and opinion of its author, and not necessarily that of the publisher or anyone associated with NMSF. No warranties or guarantees are expressed or implied by the publisher's choice to include any of the content in this volume. Neither the publisher nor the individual author(s) shall be liable for any physical, psychological, emotional, financial, or commercial damages, including, but not limited to, special, incidental, consequential or other damages. Our views and rights are the same: You are responsible for your own choices, actions, and results.

Printed in Great Britain
by Amazon